Usborne Farmyard Tales

Poppy and Sam's Baking Book

Abigail Wheatley

Illustrated by Simon Taylor-Kielty
Based on illustrations by Stephen Cartwright

Designed by Kate Rimmer

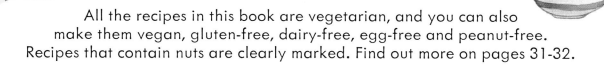

All the recipes in this book are vegetarian, and you can also make them vegan, gluten-free, dairy-free, egg-free and peanut-free. Recipes that contain nuts are clearly marked. Find out more on pages 31-32.

Contents

There is a little yellow duck for you to find on every page.

Cooking tips

Poppy and Sam live on Apple Tree Farm. They love cooking, and can do some things on their own, but a grown-up is always there to keep an eye on things. Follow the tips on these pages to cook just like Poppy and Sam.

Clean and tidy

Put on an apron and wash your hands before you start cooking.

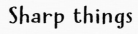

Sharp things

Some of the recipes in this book ask you to use a grater, scissors or a blunt knife. A grown-up should help children to use these safely.

Hot things

A grown-up should use oven gloves to handle hot things, while children stay back. In this book, hot things are marked with an oven glove picture, to show that a grown-up should help.

Weighing and measuring

These recipes show two types of weights. Use either, but don't swap between them in the middle of a recipe. Measure small amounts with measuring spoons.

Check that the ingredients lie level with the top of measuring spoons.

Using coconut oil

Coconut oil may be liquid on hot days, but solid on cold days. These recipes ask you to weigh out coconut oil – this works whether it's liquid or solid.

Melting things

When ingredients need melting, a grown-up can use a microwave set to full power. Using a microwave-safe bowl, heat for 20 seconds, then stir. Repeat until the ingredients melt.

Alternatively, a grown-up can melt things in a heat-proof bowl over a pan of hot water.

These brownies contain melted chocolate — you can find the recipe on pages 14-15.

Lining trays

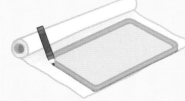

1 To line a baking tray, put it on baking paper and draw around it.

2 Snip out the shape, cutting just inside the line.

3 Then, put the shape on the tray.

Lining tins

1 To line a tin, draw around it, then cut across the whole strip, like this.

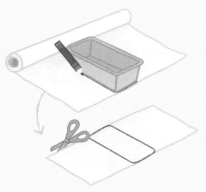

2 Turn the tin around, draw around it again, then cut out the strip.

Thin strip

Wide strip

3 Put the thin strip so its middle is in the bottom of the tin and its ends go up the tin's thin ends. Lay the wider strip on top, so its ends go up the tin's wide ends.

To make this recipe dairy-free, vegan or gluten-free, follow the instructions on page 31.

Apple flapjacks

When Poppy and Sam make these apple flapjacks, they like to use a shiny, red apple from the orchard at Apple Tree Farm.

Makes 12

Ingredients

4 tablespoons of golden syrup or maple syrup

1 teaspoon of vanilla extract

100g (4oz) butter, plant-based spread or coconut oil

1 apple

1 small banana

2 teaspoons of ground cinnamon

250g (9oz) porridge oats

100g (4oz) raisins or dried cranberries

You will also need a 20cm (8 inch) square cake tin.

1 Heat the oven to 180°C (160°C for fan ovens) or gas mark 4. Line the tin with baking paper (page 3).

2 Put the syrup, vanilla and butter, spread or coconut oil in a heatproof bowl. If you're using coconut oil and it's liquid, skip to step 4.

3 Carefully, stand the bowl over a pan of hot water and stir until the contents are melted. Or, use a microwave – see page 3.

4 Remove the bowl from the pan carefully, using oven gloves.

5 Grate the apple (but not the core) on the big holes of a grater. Add it to the syrup mixture.

6 Peel the banana and put it on a big plate. Mash it with a potato masher or fork. Add it to the mixture.

7 Add the cinnamon, oats and raisins or cranberries. Stir everything together.

Variations

You could use other dried fruit, such as dried apricots or pitted dates, snipped into small pieces.

8 Scrape the mixture into the tin. Spread it out, then smooth the top using the back of a spoon.

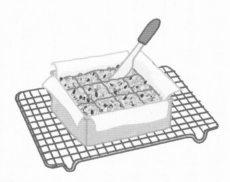

9 Bake for 30-35 minutes, until golden. Put the tin on a wire rack to cool. When it's completely cold, cut into 12 pieces using a blunt knife.

These flapjacks are crumbly because they contain so much fruit.

5

Three-colour muffins

These yummy muffins are yellow, green and red because they're made with cheese, spinach and red pepper.

To make this recipe egg-free, dairy-free, vegan or gluten-free, follow the instructions on page 31.

Ingredients

Makes 8

a little cooking oil
125g (4½oz) cheddar cheese
50g (2oz) baby spinach leaves
½ a red pepper
175g (6oz) self-raising flour
1 teaspoon of baking powder
¼ teaspoon of ground nutmeg
a pinch of black pepper
150ml (5floz or ¼ pint) milk
1 medium egg

You will also need a 12-hole deep muffin tin.

1 Heat the oven to 180°C (160°C for fan ovens) or gas mark 4. Use a paper towel to wipe a little oil inside eight holes of the muffin tray.

2 Grate the cheese on the big holes of a grater.

3 Use scissors to snip the spinach leaves into small pieces. Throw away the stalks.

4 Follow the instructions on page 11 to prepare the pepper. Then, tear it into small pieces.

5 Sift the flour and baking powder into a big bowl. Add the nutmeg and pepper. Mix well.

6 Crack the egg sharply on the rim of a bowl. Push your thumbs into the crack. Pull the shell apart so the contents slide into the bowl.

7 Put the milk in a jug. Add the egg. Mix well with a fork or whisk. Pour the mixture into the bowl.

8 Use a fork to mix everything together, until there are no pockets of flour left. It's fine if it looks lumpy.

9 Stir in the cheese, spinach and red pepper. It may look as if there's not enough flour mixture, but don't worry.

Variations

You could replace the pepper or spinach with the following ingredients:

 4 tablespoons of drained canned sweetcorn

 8 sun-dried tomatoes cut into small pieces using scissors

 50g (2oz) cooked broccoli, broken into small pieces

You could replace the cheddar with 100g (4oz) feta cheese, crumbled into small pieces, or with 75g (3oz) vegan 'cheese'.

10 Spoon the mixture into the oiled holes of the muffin tin. Bake for 20-25 minutes until risen and golden.

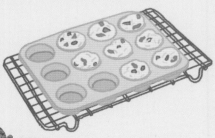

11 Put the tin on a wire rack. Leave to cool completely. Then, turn it upside down and shake the muffins out.

Peanut butter cookies

These delicious cookies are crisp on the outside and chewy in the middle. They have peanut pieces and chocolate chips inside, and scattered on top as well.

To make this recipe peanut-free, dairy-free, vegan or gluten-free, follow the instructions on page 31.

Ingredients

Makes around 12

25g (1oz) unsalted roasted peanuts
50g (2oz) butter, plant-based spread or coconut oil
60g (2½ oz) smooth peanut butter
40g (1½ oz) soft light brown sugar
40g (1½ oz) caster sugar
90g (3½ oz) plain flour
2 teaspoons of cornflour
1½ tablespoons of water
½ teaspoon of vanilla extract
25g (1oz) dark chocolate chips

You will also need 2 baking trays.

1 Heat the oven to 180°C (160°C for fan ovens) or gas mark 4. Line the trays with baking paper (page 3).

2 Put the peanuts in the middle of a clean tea towel. Fold in the edges, so the peanuts are covered. Tap gently with a rolling pin to break them into small pieces.

3 Put the butter, spread or coconut oil in a heatproof bowl. If you're using coconut oil that's liquid, skip to step 6.

4 Stand the bowl over a pan of hot water and stir until the butter, spread or coconut oil are melted. Or, use a microwave – see page 3.

5 Remove the bowl from the pan carefully, using oven gloves.

6 Put the peanut butter and both types of sugar in the bowl. Stir until you have a smooth mixture.

7 Sift the flour and cornflour into the bowl. Add the water and vanilla, half the peanuts and half the chocolate chips. Mix well.

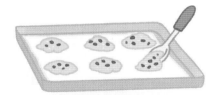

8 Scoop up a spoonful of the mixture. Drop it onto a baking tray. Do this until the mixture is used up.

Space out the spoonfuls well, as they will spread.

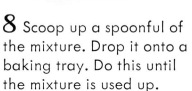

When Sam has eaten his cookie, he puts the rest in an airtight tin for later.

9 Scatter on the remaining peanuts and chocolate chips. Bake for 8-10 minutes, till golden. Leave to cool completely.

Variations

You can use almonds and almond butter, or cashew nuts and cashew nut butter, instead of the peanuts and peanut butter. Don't give these to anyone with nut allergies.

Use milk or white chocolate chips if you prefer them.

Little pizzas

Poppy likes to cook these pizzas with her friend Mia when she comes round. They're much quicker and easier to make than most pizzas, so there's plenty of time left to play.

To make this recipe dairy-free, vegan or gluten-free, follow the instructions on page 31.

Ingredients

Makes 12

For the pizza bases:
300g (11oz) self-raising flour
225ml (7½floz) plain natural yogurt, or plain plant-based 'yogurt'
1 tablespoon of olive oil

For the pizza sauce:
2 tablespoons of tomato purée
1 teaspoon of garlic purée
3 tablespoons of water
2 teaspoons of olive oil
1 teaspoon of dried oregano or dried mixed herbs

Toppings: see suggestions opposite.

You will also need 2 baking trays.

1 Heat the oven to 200°C (180 for fan ovens) or gas mark 6. Line the trays with baking paper (page 3).

2 To make the bases, put the flour, yogurt and olive oil in a big bowl. Mix with your hands.

You'll end up with 12 pieces.

3 Sprinkle some flour over a clean surface. Tip on the mixture. Pat and squeeze it into a sausage shape.

4 Split the sausage into two equal parts. Split each part into two pieces. Split each piece into three small pieces.

5 Use your hands to roll each small piece into a ball, then flatten them to make circles around 15cm (6in) across. Put them on the trays.

Pizza toppings

Here are some ideas for things you could put on top of your pizzas. You can combine them however you like.

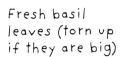 Fresh basil leaves (torn up if they are big)

 Grated hard cheese such as cheddar

Pitted black olives from a jar

Mozzarella cheese torn into small pieces

Button mushrooms wiped and snipped into small pieces

Small pieces of red (or other colour) pepper

Preparing peppers

Press with your thumbs until the stalk pops in, then tear the pepper apart.

Pull out the seeds, stalk and white parts.

Tear the rest into pieces.

6 Bake for 5 minutes. Take out of the oven and leave to cool. Turn the oven down to 180°C (160°C for fan ovens) or gas mark 4.

7 Now, make the sauce. Put the tomato purée, garlic purée, water, oil and oregano or herbs in a small bowl. Mix well.

8 When the bases are cold, spoon some sauce onto each one. Spread it out with the back of the spoon.

9 Sprinkle over your chosen toppings. You can use different toppings for each pizza if you like.

10 Bake for 10 minutes, or until the bases are golden at the edges.

Blueberry scones

Sam can mix these scones all by himself, just by stirring coconut milk into flour. If there's no coconut milk in the cupboard, Mrs Boot uses milk and butter instead – find out how in 'Variations' on the opposite page.

To make this recipe dairy-free, vegan or gluten-free, follow the instructions on page 31.

1 Heat the oven to 220°C (200°C for fan ovens) or gas mark 7. Line the tray with baking paper (page 3).

Makes around 8

Ingredients

175g (6oz) self-raising flour
½ teaspoon of baking powder
1½ tablespoons of caster sugar
8 tablespoons of coconut milk
50g (2oz) fresh blueberries
a little milk or plant-based 'milk', for brushing

You will also need a baking tray and a 6cm (2½in) round cutter.

2 Sift the flour and baking powder into a big bowl. Add the sugar and stir it in.

3 Mix in the coconut milk, until you have a soft dough.

4 Add the blueberries. Stir them in really gently, trying not to squash them.

5 Dust a clean surface with flour. Tip on the dough. Use your hands to pat it into a ball.

6 Dust a rolling pin with flour. Put the dough on the surface and roll it out.

Stop when the dough is twice as thick as your little finger.

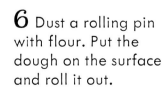

7 Use the cutter to cut out lots of circles.

8 Squeeze the scraps into a ball. Roll it out and cut more circles, until it's all used up.

A 6cm (2½in) cutter makes little scones, but you can use a bigger cutter.

9 Put the circles on the baking tray. Brush the tops with the milk.

 10 Bake for 8-10 minutes, until risen and golden. Put the tray on a wire rack to cool completely.

Variations

Instead of coconut milk, use 50g (2oz) butter and 5 tablespoons of milk. Put the butter in a heatproof bowl over a pan of hot water. Stir until it melts (or use a microwave – see page 3).

Remove the bowl carefully using oven gloves. Leave to cool for 5 minutes, then stir in the milk. Add at step 3.

Little chocolate brownies

These delicious, squidgy brownies contain lots of yummy things including chia seeds. Watch how they soak up water to make a sticky gel, which helps to glue the brownies together.

To make this recipe dairy-free, vegan or gluten-free, follow the instructions on page 31.

Makes 10

1 Heat the oven to 180°C (160°C for fan ovens) or gas mark 4. Line the tin with baking paper (page 3).

Ingredients

1 tablespoon of chia seeds
4 tablespoons of cold water
40g (1½oz) pitted prunes
50g (2oz) dark or milk chocolate
20g (¾oz) butter or
   plant-based spread
100g (4oz) caster sugar
½ teaspoon of vanilla extract
50g (2oz) self-raising flour
1 teaspoon of cocoa powder
1 tablespoon of chocolate chips

You will also need a 900g (2lb) loaf tin, measuring around 20x12x8cm (8x5x3½in).

2 Put the chia seeds in a cup. Pour over the cold water. Set aside.

3 Put the prunes in a cup. Pour over enough hot water to cover them. Set aside.

4 Put the butter or spread in a large heatproof bowl. Break the 50g (2oz) of chocolate on top.

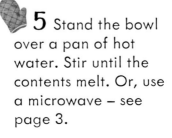

5 Stand the bowl over a pan of hot water. Stir until the contents melt. Or, use a microwave – see page 3.

6 Remove the bowl from the pan carefully, using oven gloves.

7 Drain the prunes in a sieve, then put them back in the cup. Use scissors to snip them into small pieces.

8 Put the prunes, sugar, vanilla and the chia mixture in the bowl. Mix well.

Variations

You could use dark, milk or white chocolate chips if you like.

9 Sift the flour and cocoa powder into the bowl. Mix them in gently, moving the spoon in the shape of a number 8.

10 Pour the mixture into the tin. Sprinkle over the chocolate chips. Bake for 25-30 minutes.

11 Poke a skewer or cocktail stick into the middle. If it comes out clean, it's cooked. If not, bake for 10 minutes more then test again.

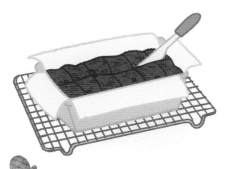

12 Put the tin on a wire rack to cool. When it's completely cold, cut into 10 squares using a blunt knife.

These brownies were made with dark chocolate and dark chocolate chips.

Filo fruit tarts

Poppy and Sam make these tarts to eat in the garden on warm days. Filo pastry makes light and crispy bases, filled with cool yogurt and sweet summer berries.

To make this recipe dairy-free, vegan or gluten-free, follow the instructions on page 31.

Ingredients

Makes 9

4 sheets of filo pastry

a little sunflower oil or other light cooking oil

150g (5oz) plain Greek-style yogurt or plain plant-based Greek-style 'yogurt'

50g (2oz) raspberries

1 tablespoon of maple syrup or honey

300g (11oz) mixed berries such as strawberries, raspberries, blueberries and blackberries

You will also need a 12-hole fairy cake or bun tin.

1 Heat the oven to 180°C (160°C for fan ovens) or gas mark 4.

2 Lay two sheets of filo on top of each other on a clean surface. Snip into three strips.

3 Then snip across to make nine squares, like this.

4 Repeat steps 2 and 3 with the remaining two sheets of filo.

5 Brush a little oil into nine holes of the cake tin.

6 Pick up both layers of a filo square. Lay it in a hole of the tin. Do this again until nine holes are filled.

7 Brush a little oil over the edges of the filo that stick out around the hole.

8 Lay another two-layer square of filo in each hole of the in. Repeat step 7.

9 Bake for 6-8 minutes until crisp and golden. Leave to cool.

10 Meanwhile, put the 50g (2oz) of raspberries in a bowl. Mash with a fork to squash them, then stir in the yogurt and the syrup or honey.

11 If you're using strawberries, pull out the green stalks. Snip any large strawberries in half.

12 Lift the pastry cases out of the tray. Spoon a little yogurt mixture into each, then scatter on some mixed berries.

Variations

If it's not the season for fresh berries, use tinned fruit such as peaches or apricots, patted dry with kitchen paper and snipped into bite-sized chunks.

Little carrot cakes

When there are fresh carrots in the Apple Tree Farm garden, Poppy and Sam like to grate them and make them into these little carrot cakes with a yummy yogurt topping.

To make this recipe nut-free, dairy-free, vegan or gluten-free, follow the instructions on page 31.

Makes 12

Ingredients

For the cakes:
175g (6oz) carrots
75g (3oz) walnut pieces (optional)
100g (4oz) soft light brown sugar
50g (2oz) sultanas
175g (6oz) self-raising flour
2 teaspoons of ground cinnamon
½ teaspoon of ground nutmeg
100ml (3½ floz) sunflower oil or
    other light vegetable oil
6 tablespoons of water

For the yogurt topping:
300ml (10floz) plain Greek-style
    yogurt or plain plant-based
    Greek-style 'yogurt'
4 teaspoons of maple syrup
    or honey

You will also need a 12-hole deep muffin tin and 12 paper muffin cases.

1 Heat the oven to 180°C (160°C for fan ovens) or gas mark 4. Put a paper case in each hole of the muffin tin.

2 Grate the carrots on the big holes of a grater. Stop when you get near the top of the carrot.

3 Put the grated carrot in a big bowl. Mix in the walnuts (if using), sugar, sultanas, flour, cinnamon and nutmeg.

4 Pour in the oil and water. Mix well. The mixture will look quite wet, but this is fine.

5 Spoon the mixture into the paper cases. Bake for 35 minutes, until risen and brown.

6 Put the tin on a wire rack. Leave to cool completely.

7 For the yogurt topping, put the yogurt and syrup or honey in a bowl. Mix well.

The paper cases have been peeled off these cakes, so they're ready to eat.

Spoon on a dollop of topping just before eating a cake.

Variations

If you don't like nuts, just leave them out.

These cakes are delicious eaten without any topping.

Pastry snails

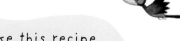

These pastry snails are Sam's favourite thing to cook on rainy days. He likes to use green pesto, but red pesto looks great too.

To make this recipe nut-free, dairy-free, vegan or gluten-free, follow the instructions on page 31.

1 Take the pastry out of the fridge. Leave at room temperature for 30 minutes.

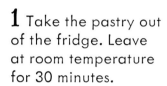

2 Line the tray with baking paper – see page 3. Heat the oven to 220°C (200°C for fan ovens) or gas mark 7.

Ingredients

Makes around 15

a pack of ready-rolled puff pastry (around 300g or 11oz)

4 teaspoons of green or red pesto from a jar

You will also need a baking tray and a clean 30cm (12in) ruler.

3 Unroll the pastry. Leave it on its paper wrapper. Dust the ruler with flour. Press it into the pastry like this, to make three equal strips.

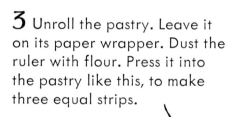

4 Put one pastry strip on a surface dusted with flour.

Roll up the others in their paper wrappers, seal and freeze for another day.

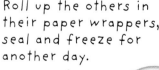

5 Divide the pastry strip into 1cm (½in) strips like this, by pressing the ruler into the pastry again and again.

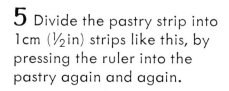

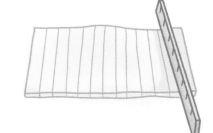

6 Spread the pesto onto the pastry with the back of a spoon, leaving a 2cm (1in) gap at one end of the strips.

Gap

Variations

If you're not keen on pesto, you could use the same amount of sundried tomato purée instead. Or, use your favourite flavour of jam, to make sweet pastry snails.

7 Put a little cold water in a cup. Dip in a finger. Run the finger along the gap with no pesto, to wet it.

Roll this way

8 Roll up each little strip from the pesto-covered end, to make a spiral. Put it on the tray.

Some of these were made using green pesto, and some with red pesto.

9 Bake for 10-12 minutes, until puffy and golden.

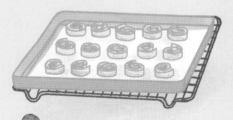

10 Put the tray on a wire rack. Leave to cool completely.

Gingerbread people

Everyone loves gingerbread people, but if you don't have a person-shaped cutter to make them, just use any other shape of cutter – your biscuits will be just as delicious.

To make this recipe dairy-free, vegan or gluten-free, follow the instructions on page 31.

Makes 9 big biscuits

Ingredients

125g (4½oz) softened butter or plant-based 'butter' from a block
100g (4oz) soft dark brown sugar
5 tablespoons of golden syrup
175g (6oz) wholemeal flour
150g (5oz) plain flour
2 teaspoons of ground ginger
1 teaspoon of mixed spice
1 teaspoon of bicarbonate of soda

You will also need 2 baking trays, a cookie cutter and a cocktail stick.

1 Heat the oven to 180°C (160°C for fan ovens) or gas mark 4. Line the trays with baking paper (page 3).

2 Put the butter and sugar in a big bowl. Use your hands to squeeze and mix them together.

3 Use your hands to beat the mixture again and again until it's light and fluffy.

4 Add the syrup, flour, ginger, spice and bicarbonate of soda. Mix everything together.

5 Use your hands to squash and squeeze the mixture into a smooth ball.

Squash it against the bowl.

6 Sprinkle a little flour over a surface and a rolling pin.

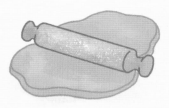

7 Roll out the dough until it's a little thinner than a pencil.

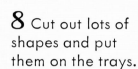

8 Cut out lots of shapes and put them on the trays.

9 Squeeze the scraps together, cut out more shapes and put them on the trays.

10 Use the cocktail stick to poke holes for faces or other decorations.

11 Bake for 10-12 minutes, until slightly browned.

12 Leave to cool completely.

Variations

This recipe uses a mixture of plain and wholemeal flour, but you could use just plain, or just wholemeal.

Soda bread rolls

Soda bread is a type of quick bread recipe that's popular in Ireland. Mr Boot taught Poppy and Sam this recipe, and showed them how to snip the top of the bread. Stories say this is to let out any fairies stuck in the dough.

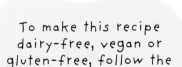

To make this recipe dairy-free, vegan or gluten-free, follow the instructions on page 32.

Makes 8

Ingredients

175g (6oz) plain flour (plus extra for sprinkling)
175g (6oz) wholemeal flour
65g (1½oz) rolled oats (plus extra for sprinkling)
1 teaspoon of salt
1 teaspoon of bicarbonate of soda
275ml (1¼ pints) milk or plant-based 'milk'
1 tablespoon of lemon juice
2 tablespoons of sunflower oil or other light cooking oil
a little water for brushing

You will also need a baking tray.

1 Heat the oven to 180°C (160°C for fan oven) or gas mark 4. Sprinkle a little flour on the tray.

2 Sift both types of flour into a large bowl. Add the oats, salt and bicarbonate of soda.

3 Put the lemon juice, milk and oil in a jug. Mix well.

4 Pour the liquid into the big bowl. Stir it in.

5 Use your hands to pat and squash the mixture into a ball.

6 Sprinkle a little flour on a clean surface. Put the ball on the surface.

7 Divide the ball into 8 equal pieces. Roll each piece into a ball.

Space them out well.

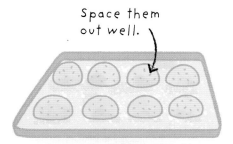

8 Put the balls on the tray. Press each one slightly, to flatten it a little.

Do this on each ball.

9 Use scissors to snip a line across the top of a ball.

Snip an X on each ball.

10 Then, make two more snips, to make an 'X' shape.

11 Brush a little water over the top of each one, then sprinkle on some oats.

12 Bake for 20-25 mins. Leave on the tray to cool completely.

Pumpkin seed oatcakes

Because of the pumpkin seeds in these savoury oatcakes, Poppy and Sam like to cut them out with a pumpkin-shaped cookie cutter – but you could use any cutter you like.

To make this recipe seed-free, dairy-free, vegan or gluten-free, follow the instructions on page 32.

Ingredients

Makes around 20

75g (3oz) porridge oats
75g (3oz) wholemeal flour
a pinch of salt
25g (1oz) pumpkin seeds
15g (½oz) butter or plant-based 'butter' from a block
75ml (3floz) warm water

You will also need 2 baking trays and a cookie cutter.

1 Heat the oven to 180°C (160°C for fan ovens) or gas mark 4. Line the trays with baking paper (page 3).

2 Put the oats in a big bowl. Add the flour, salt and pumpkin seeds.

3 Put the water in a jug. Add the butter. Stir until the butter melts.

4 Pour the water mixture into the bowl. Mix everything together well.

5 Use your hands to squash and squeeze the mixture into a ball.

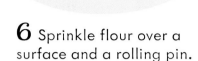

6 Sprinkle flour over a surface and a rolling pin.

7 Roll out the dough until it is half as thick as a pencil.

Place the cutter so it's not cutting through any pumpkin seeds, as they can be tough.

8 Cut out lots of shapes. Put them on the trays.

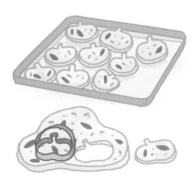

9 Squeeze the scraps together, cut out more shapes and put them on the trays.

10 Bake for 12-15 minutes, until slightly browned. Leave to cool completely.

Variations

Instead of flour, you could use oat flour – make it by pulsing 75g (3oz) oats in a food processor.

If you're allergic to seeds, just leave them out.

Savoury star biscuits

These tasty little biscuits are perfect for parties. The main recipe is for cheesy biscuits but there are other flavours to try, and you could use a different shape of cutter too.

To make this recipe dairy-free, vegan or gluten-free, follow the instructions on page 32.

Ingredients

Makes 20-30

100g (4oz) cheddar cheese
50g (2oz) softened butter or plant-based 'butter' from a block
100g (4oz) self-raising flour
25ml (1floz) cold milk or plant-based 'milk'
½ teaspoon of smoked paprika (optional)
a pinch of ground black pepper

You will also need 2 baking trays and a small cookie cutter.

1 Heat the oven to 180°C (160°C for fan ovens) or gas mark 4. Line the trays with baking paper (page 3).

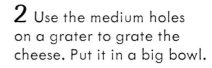

2 Use the medium holes on a grater to grate the cheese. Put it in a big bowl.

3 Put the butter in the bowl. Use a fork to mash and mix it into the cheese.

4 Put the flour, milk, paprika (if using), and pepper in the bowl.

5 Use your hands to squash and mix everything together into a smooth ball.

28

6 Sprinkle a little flour over a clean surface and a rolling pin. Put the dough on the surface.

7 Roll out the dough until it is around as thick as a pencil.

8 Cut out lots of shapes and put them on the trays.

9 Squash the scraps together, roll them out and cut more stars, until the dough is used up.

10 Bake for 12 minutes, until golden. Leave on the tray to cool completely.

Variations

You can leave out the cheese and try one of these flavours instead...

For tomato stars, you will need 1 tablespoon of sundried tomato purée. Skip steps 2 and 3. Put the butter in a bowl, add the purée, then continue from step 4.

For yeast extract spread stars, you will need 1½ teaspoons of yeast extract spread. Leave out the paprika. Skip steps 2 and 3. Put the butter in a bowl, add the yeast extract spread, then continue from step 4.

Best banana bread

This banana bread is one of Poppy's favourite things to make – she really enjoys mashing the bananas.

1 Heat the oven to 180°C (160°C for fan ovens) or gas mark 4. Line the tin with baking paper (page 3).

2 Peel the bananas and put them on a big plate. Mash with a fork or potato masher.

3 Put the mashed banana in a big bowl. Add the oil and sugar and mix well.

4 Sift over the flour, cinnamon, mixed spice and baking powder. Mix well.

5 Add the raisins, then stir them in.

6 Scrape the mixture into the tin. Bake for 30 minutes.

7 Poke a skewer or cocktail stick into the middle. If it comes out clean, it's cooked. If not, bake for 10 minutes more then test again.

To make this recipe dairy-free, vegan or gluten-free, follow the instructions on page 32.

Ingredients

3 very ripe bananas
75ml (3floz) sunflower or other light cooking oil
100g (4oz) dark brown sugar
225g (8oz) self-raising flour
2 teaspoons of baking powder
2 teaspoons of ground cinnamon
2 teaspoons of mixed spice
40g (1½oz) raisins (optional)

You will also need a 900g (2lb) loaf tin, measuring around 20x12x8cm (8x5x3½in).

8 Leave in the tin to cool completely. Slice with a blunt knife.

Help with swapping ingredients

All the recipes in this book are already vegetarian, but you can make them vegan, peanut-free, gluten-free, egg-free and/or dairy-free (or any combination of these) using the instructions that follow. Recipes containing nuts and peanuts are clearly marked.

If you're cooking for someone with special dietary requirements, always check packaged ingredients such as flour, baking powder, margarine or vanilla extract, in case they contain anything unsuitable.

Apple flapjacks

To make this recipe dairy-free and/or vegan, use plant-based spread or coconut oil. To make it gluten-free, use gluten-free oats.

Three-colour muffins

To make this recipe dairy-free, replace the milk with plant-based 'milk' and leave out the cheese or replace it with vegan 'cheese'. To make it egg-free, before you start, mix 1 tablespoon of chia seeds with 3 tablespoons of water and set aside, then add in place of the egg in step 6. To make it vegan, see above to make it dairy-free and egg-free. To make it gluten-free, use gluten-free self-raising flour and gluten-free baking powder.

Peanut butter cookies

To make this recipe peanut-free, use almonds or cashews instead – see 'Variations' on page 9. Please note these contain nuts. To make it dairy-free and/or vegan, use plant-based spread or coconut oil, and use dairy-free/plant-based chocolate chips. To make it gluten-free, use gluten-free flour.

Little pizzas

To make this recipe dairy-free and/or vegan, use plant-based 'yogurt' and avoid cheese toppings, or use vegan 'cheese' instead. To make it gluten-free, use gluten-free self-raising flour.

Blueberry scones

To make this recipe dairy-free and/or vegan, use plant-based 'milk'. To make it gluten-free, use gluten-free self-raising flour and gluten-free baking powder. If you want to replace the coconut milk, see 'Variations' on page 13 to use butter and milk instead.

Little chocolate brownies

To make this recipe dairy-free and/or vegan, use dairy-free/plant-based chocolate and cocoa powder, and plant-based spread. To make it gluten-free, use gluten-free self-raising flour.

Filo fruit tarts

To make this recipe dairy-free and/or vegan, use plant-based 'yogurt' and maple syrup. To make it gluten-free, replace the filo pastry with one sheet of ready-rolled gluten-free shortcrust pastry and lay it on a clean surface; snip it into 9 squares, then follow step 5 and place a square of pastry in each hole. Follow steps 9-12 as normal.

Little carrot cakes

To make this recipe nut-free, leave out the nuts. To make it dairy-free, use plant-based Greek-style 'yogurt' for the topping. To make it vegan, use plant-based Greek-style 'yogurt' and maple syrup for the topping. To make it gluten-free, use gluten-free self-raising flour.

Pastry snails

To make this recipe nut-free, use a 'free from nuts' type of pesto, or use sundried tomato purée or jam – see 'Variations' on page 21. To make it dairy-free and/or vegan, use plant-based pastry and plant-based pesto, or swap the pesto for sundried tomato purée or jam. To make it gluten-free, use gluten-free puff pastry.

Gingerbread people

To make this recipe dairy-free and/or vegan, use plant-based 'butter'. To make it gluten-free, use gluten-free flour.

Help with swapping ingredients (continued)

Soda bread rolls

To make this recipe dairy-free and/or vegan, use plant-based 'milk'. To make it gluten-free, use gluten-free oats and gluten-free flour; you will also need to add 2 teaspoons of gluten-free baking powder at step 2.

Pumpkin seed oatcakes

To make this recipe seed-free, leave out the pumpkin seeds. To make it dairy-free and/or vegan, use plant-based 'butter'. To make it gluten-free, use gluten-free oats; swap the flour for gluten-free flour, or use oat flour – see 'Variations' on page 27.

Savoury star biscuits

To make this recipe dairy-free and/or vegan, leave out the cheese, use plant-based 'butter' and plant-based 'milk'; see 'Variations' on page 29 for instructions on replacing the cheese with sundried tomato purée or yeast extract spread. To make the recipe gluten-free, use gluten-free self-raising flour.

Best banana bread

To make this recipe gluten-free, use gluten-free self-raising flour and gluten-free baking powder.

Index

Home economist: Maud Eden   Photography by Abigail Wheatley   Series editor: Sam Taplin
Digital imaging by Keith Furnival   Step-by-step illustrations by Claire Thomas